One Light One Love

Sharon Warren

ONE LIGHT, ONE LOVE
by Sharon Warren

For information address
IMAGE CONCEPTS & MORE
P.O. Box 230144
Portland, Oregon 97281-0144

FIRST EDITION
1st Printing

Library of Congress
catalog card number 93-77186

ISBN # 0-9636074-0-5

PRINTED IN
THE UNITED STATES OF AMERICA
10 9 8 7 6 5 4 3 2

Printed on
Recycled
Paper

DEDICATION

I dedicate this book to the memory of my beloved grandparents, Ira and Murle Smith, who taught me about life and love. To my parents, Howard and Thelma Smith, thank you for loving me and caring through all these years. To Scott, Christina and Michelle, my precious children, thanks for being wise beyond your years and for never giving up on me through all the hard times. Deep appreciation to the gentle "knight" who guided my growth and whose love and wisdom inspired these poems and who lovingly edited and proofread the manuscript. Finally, I dedicate *One Light, One Love* to my first grandchild, who is already much loved.

CONTENTS

ACKNOWLEDGEMENTS

This book is a reality because of the following people whose love and encouragement nurtured the vision of "One Light, One Love", a gift to the world.

Many "BEAU-TEE-FUL" thanks to Elsie Petrequin, the artist. Her passion, playfulness, inspiration and talent have added a heavenly dimension to this book. Your friendship, love and guidance have led me toward a greater awareness of the truth.

My gratitude to Carol Guthrie, the graphic designer, who was divinely sent to us and who shared our vision. Her love, dedication, talent and experience made our work a labor of "Love".

Thank you to Nancy Middlebrook, my friend and "teacher', who stood by me through many "storms of life" and taught me to believe in myself. Joyous gratitude I extend to you for your love, support and vision of the cover design.

My loving appreciation for the companionship and guidance of my precious friend, LaVon Richards, who has loved me unconditionally. Your "knowing" guided the final selection of the poems in this manuscript.

Much love and appreciation to Roberta Jarrett, the author of *Caring For The Caregiver*, whose words of "knowing" gave me the courage to take a "leap of faith".

Heartfelt thanks to Berdell Moffett, the publishing consultant, whose warmth, caring, and precious experience were invaluable in teaching me how to self-publish.

Deep love and appreciation to my "wonder-full" friends who loved the manuscript and "gems of wisdom". You believed in the value of the poems and the "loving" spirit residing therein.

To Rev. Mary Manin Boggs, co-creator of the Living Enrichment Center, located in Wilsonville, Oregon, my gratitude for her inspirational guidance. Mary Boggs, through the Living Enrichment Center, "nourishes" and, "heals lives and builds dreams". This was done for me. LEC does this for countless others and is doing it each day throughout the world. Carry the Word . . . give the Love . . . receive the Spirit.

Many thanks to Betty Steflik and Julie Lay who contributed to Elsie Petrequin's biography.

I am especially grateful to all the men and women who have been my "teachers" over the years. Their words have touched my heart and fed my soul. The list includes Robert Frost, Ralph Waldo Emerson, Richard Bach, Wayne Dyer and Marianne Williamson. My love and gratitude to my high school English teacher, Richard Ault.

Praise to my "Knight of Light" for his "Gems of Wisdom". He wrote my biography, proofread the final manuscript and supplied inspiration, love and joyous support every step of the way.

PREFACE

I grew up in a blue-collar, middle-class family on a small farm in Michigan. My childhood memories include: playing with dolls under the big apple tree behind our house; the smell of freshly-cut hay and homemade bread; the taste of fresh, garden tomatoes and crisp Transparent apples; the feel of thick green grass under my, almost always, bare feet; the sound of crunchy snow, crickets, thunder and rain; and the beauty of lightning, fireflies, fluffy white clouds, forsythia and lilacs.

Much of my spare time was spent in Grandma Smith's kitchen or somewhere out on the forty acres with one of my beloved grandparents or two younger brothers-frolicking, playing and living.

Throughout high school and college while studying English Literature; Emerson, Browning, Thoreau, Shakespeare, the Bible, Frost, etc., I came to love poetry and began writing both poetry and prose to express the wonder of life and feel the beauty of it.

With the deaths of my precious grandfather, President Kennedy, Bobby Kennedy, Martin Luther King, Jr., and finally the sudden and traumatic accidental death of an admired personal friend, Bruce Walker, I then embarked on a major life transition. I felt like a caterpillar who was wrapped in a hard, dark cocoon and that I would die if I couldn't get out.

The poems in this collection resulted from nearly a half century of love which I learned from all the people in my life: my parents, grandparents, brothers, friends, extended family and the gentle man whom I had searched for my entire life.

After a second divorce, I started receiving counseling to begin recovery from co-dependence. I was guided to journal my experiences and feelings to assist in the healing process. I also found The Living Enrichment Center, a 10-year old New Thought church and found a home where I had support for my journey. The first Sunday that I entered the Westgate Theater, which served as the Sanctuary, I felt as though I had walked in to a "sea of love". I was finally home . . . no longer alone. I began to know on a conscious level what I had always known . . . we are never ALONE . . . we are ALL ONE when we are aware of Love.

Through the recovery process and the examination of my life, I was sent many "angels" to guide my awakening. One of them appeared only days after I had written down a list of qualities I wanted in my dream relationship. His presence, words, music and sense of humor began, after a few months, inspiring this poetry. I was learning, growing, and healing through his words. I recorded these "gems of wisdom" and his loving guidance, which served as my lessons and became a mirror to my knowing of who I really am. Through our growing relationship, I came to understand that we are all "one light and one love". Most of the poems came through me in the middle of the night, or early morning as I awoke, and I recorded them in my journals which were by my bed.

We are, each one of us, all capable and deserving of an infinite amount of joy, peace and abundance. All we need to do is to **DESIRE** it, then **ACT AS IF** we already have it, and **SO IT IS!** When I began to learn that I could create anything I truly wanted, as long as it was for my higher good and the higher good for all concerned, I only had to **BELIEVE** and **LET GO.** Receiving and creating become effortless when we let go and trust in the process.

So here, I give to you, my praise to the Spirit and Love that has kept me so warm and embraced in the peace and wonder of life. It is my loving hope that you too will find the strength and inspiration to see new facets to your world; to seek out the gems of wisdom that God places so carefully within us; to "hear" the special "angels" that guide us to be open to the "wonder-full-ness" of life, all through *One Light, One Love.*

Sharon Warren
Portland, Oregon
February 1993

FOREWORD

In this work, poet Sharon Warren has captured the essence of Divine love as it is expressed through human hearts.

God is love - love is God. Simple but profound. Timely and yet eternal. Old but every day new in the hearts and minds of people who have opened themselves to the bliss of human love, freely expressed and joyfully accepted. Eternity and beauty in the moment.

This book is a gift for the ages!

Roberta Jarrett
Author of *Caring For The Caregiver,*
"A Nurse's Journey to Health and Inner Peace"

One Light One Love

Sharon Warren

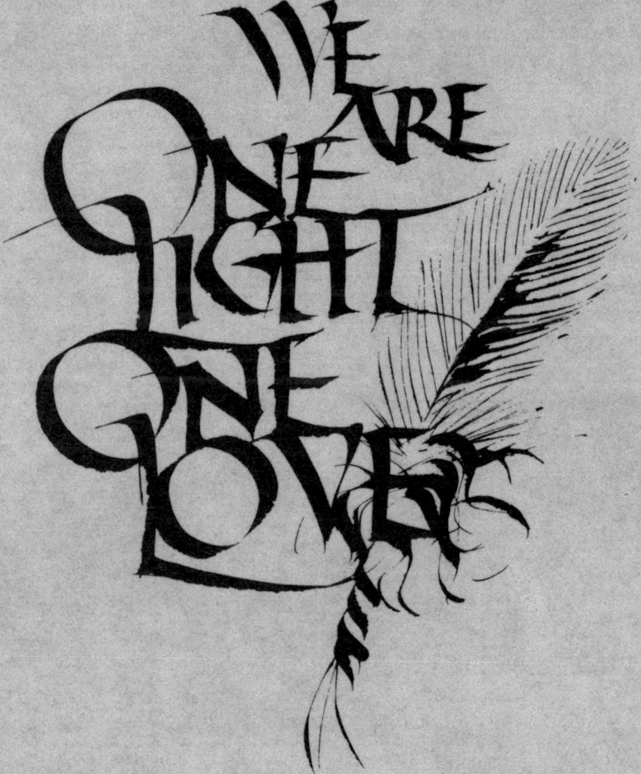
WE ARE
ONE
LIGHT
ONE
LOVER

I am not yours
You are not mine
To own
    To possess
And so it is
I can not lose you
You can not lose me
We are
    One Light
        One Love

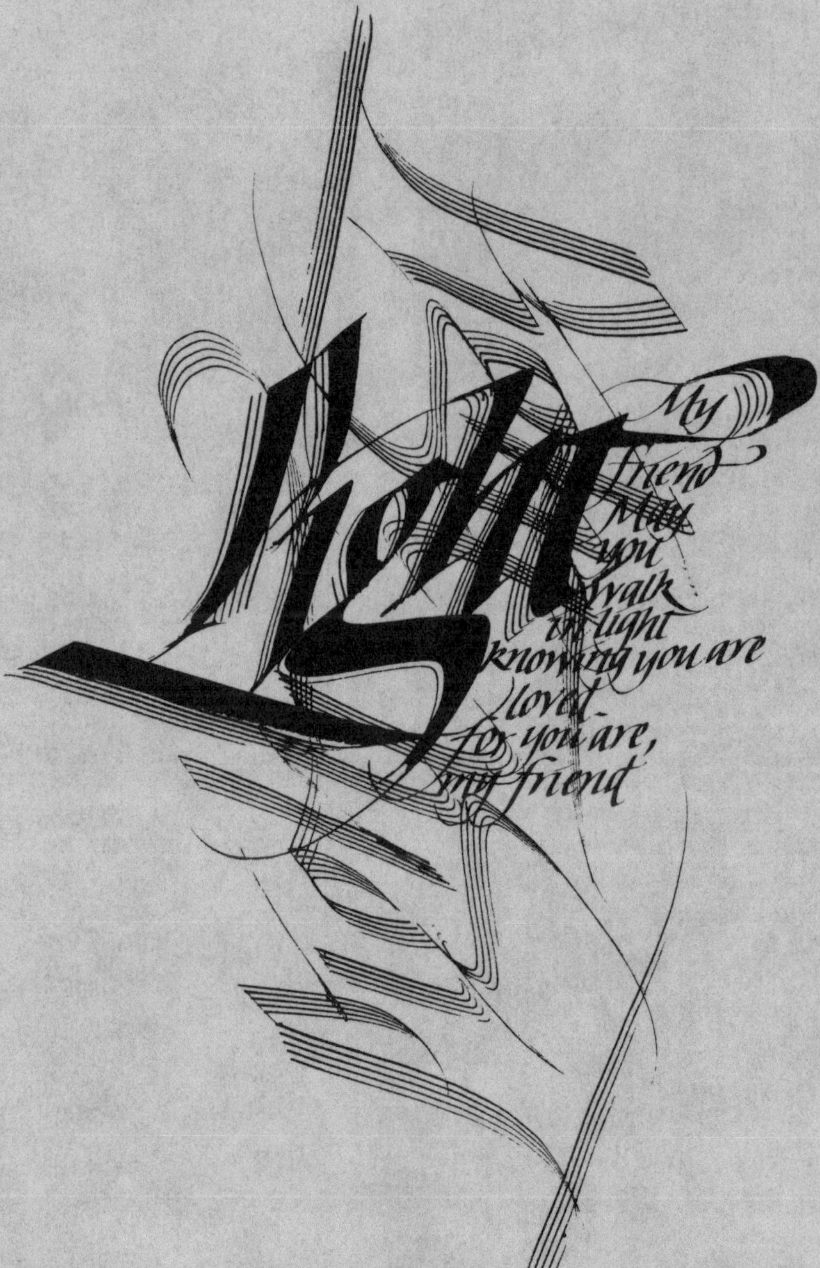
My
friend
May
you
walk
in light
knowing you are
loved
for you are,
my friend

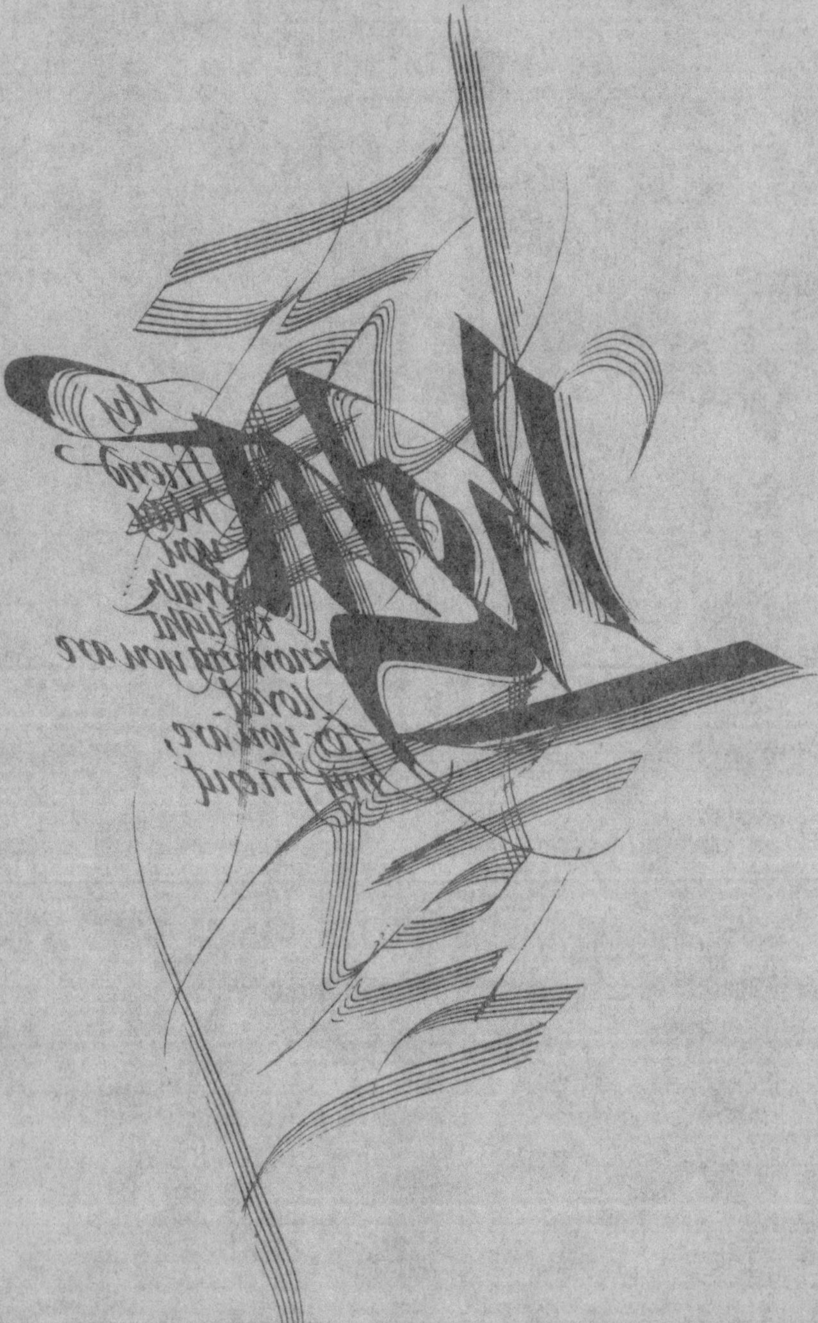

MY FRIEND

Wherever you may go
In this life and beyond
May you walk
In the Light
Knowing you are loved.
For you are my Friend,
A warm and gentle spirit
Bringing Love and laughter
To all who meet you.
Your life is a gift
You share with the world
And my life is richer
Because I have known you.

Eternal
Light
Love

Flows through me
And I am one
With the Earth
The Sky
The Sun
And all that is
Eternal Light and
Love
Unconditional
and
Infinite

Eternal Light and Love
Flows through me
And I am One
With the earth
    The Sky
        The Sun
And all that is

Eternal Light and Love
Unconditional and infinite
Heals my body
Feeds my Soul
    My Mind
        My Spirit

Eternal Light and Love
Flows through me
And Nourishes
    One and all.

ONE

Two souls forever joined
in Universal Love

No space
No time
Separate
Two souls
Forever joined
In
Universal
Love

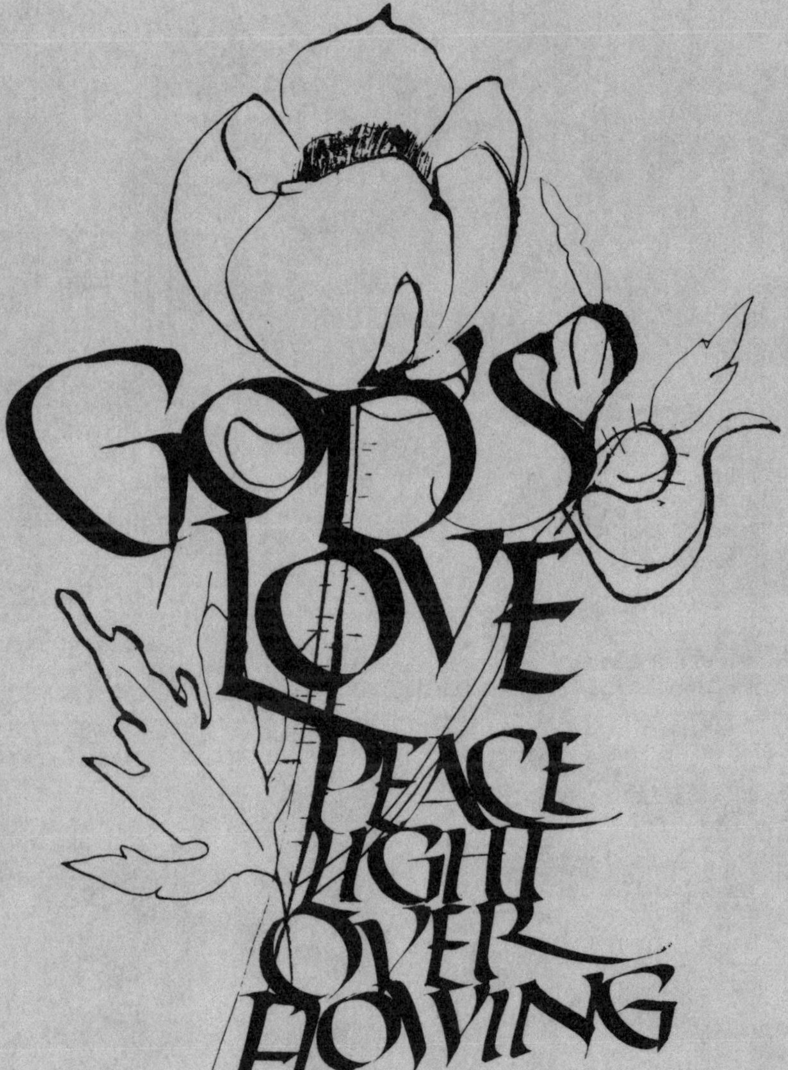
GOD'S
LOVE
PEACE
LIGHT
OVER
FLOWING

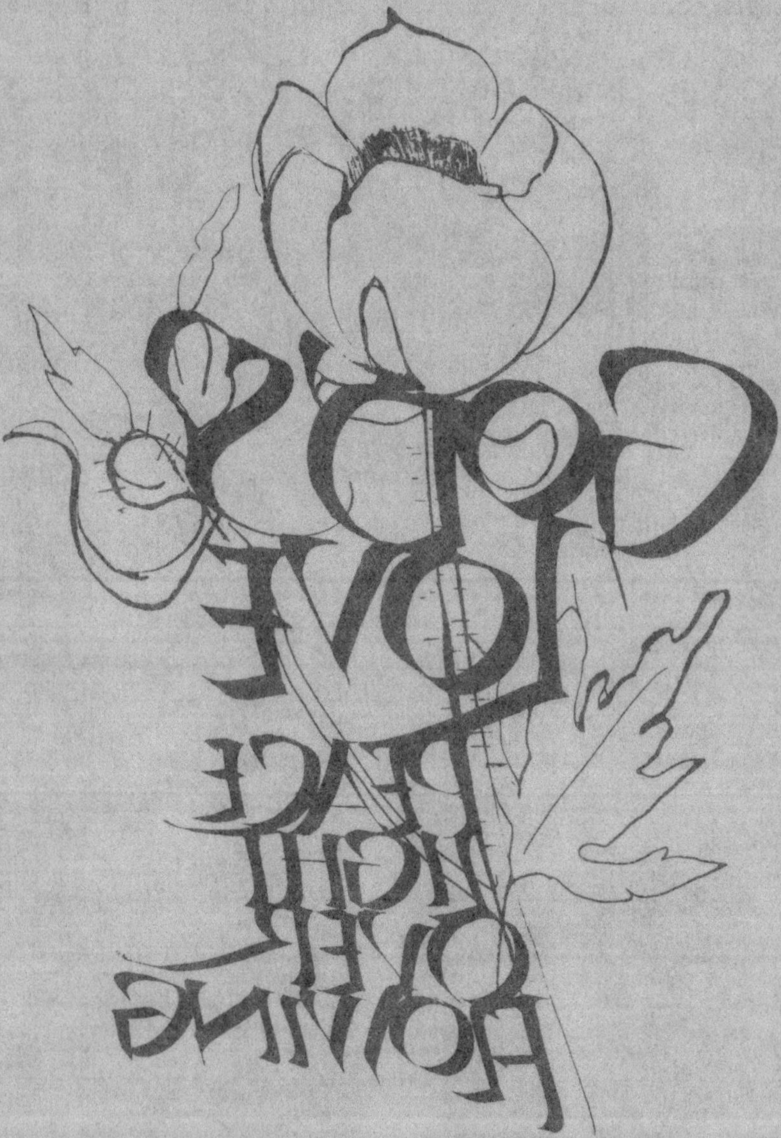
GOD'S
LOVE
PEACE
MIGHT
OVER
FLOWING

He sings to me
He holds me
He looks into my eyes

He talks with me
He teaches me
He touches me inside

He trusts me
He cares for me
He gives me peace and Light

He hears me
He supports me
He lets me be myself

He warms me
He loves me
He fills to overflowing

He shares
    He smiles
        He is

God's Love

Behold
Heaven
Light
of
God
in
my
hands

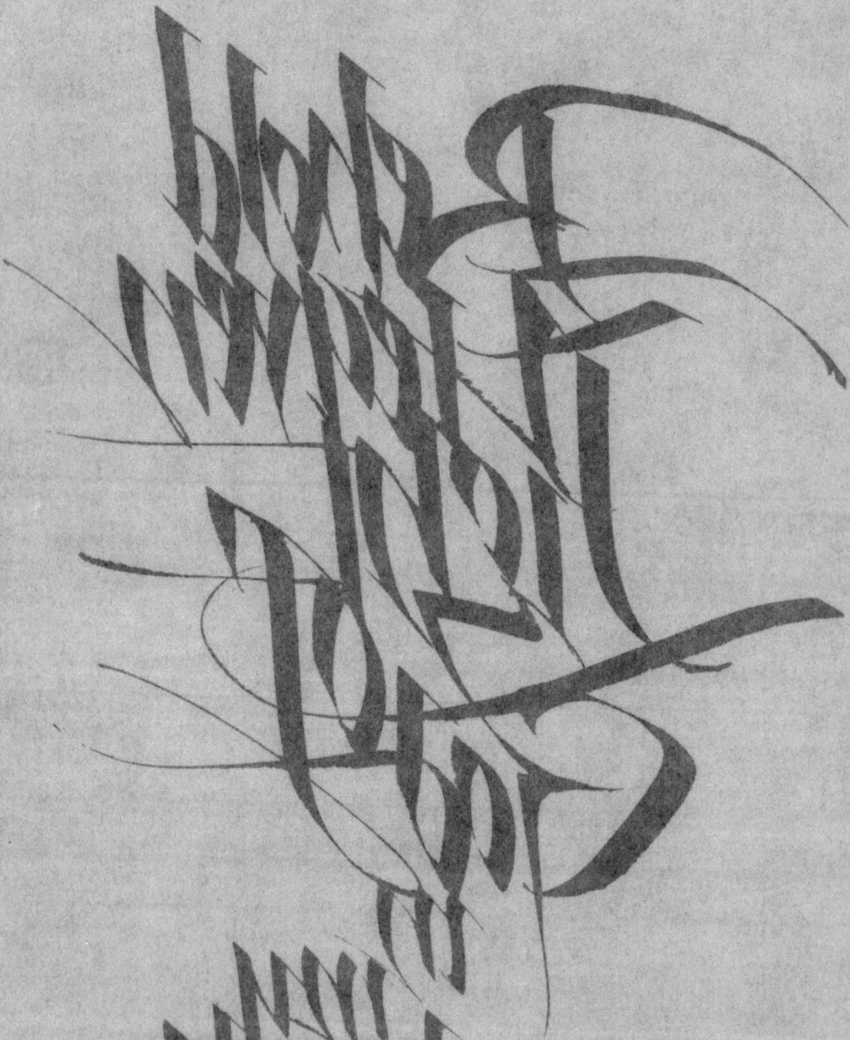

Behold Heaven
The Light of God
In my hands
Your face
Precious gift
Treasure
Of my Soul
Be free
To walk thy path
In Love
In peace

You are a
diamond
I am one, too.
You sparkle,
you shine
Bright,
warm
and
true,
Each facet
shows
a new side
of you

You are a diamond
I am one too.
You sparkle, you shine
Bright, warm and true

Each facet shows
A new side of you
That I've never seen
'Til your Light shines through

A clown, a poet
A child, the wind
A guru, a scholar
A lover, a friend

A man, a boy
A wizard, a musician
An oak tree, a willow
A knight, Peter Pan

Each moment with you
Is revealed unto me
A miracle, the facets
Of you shining on me.

Music To My Soul

The beat of your heart

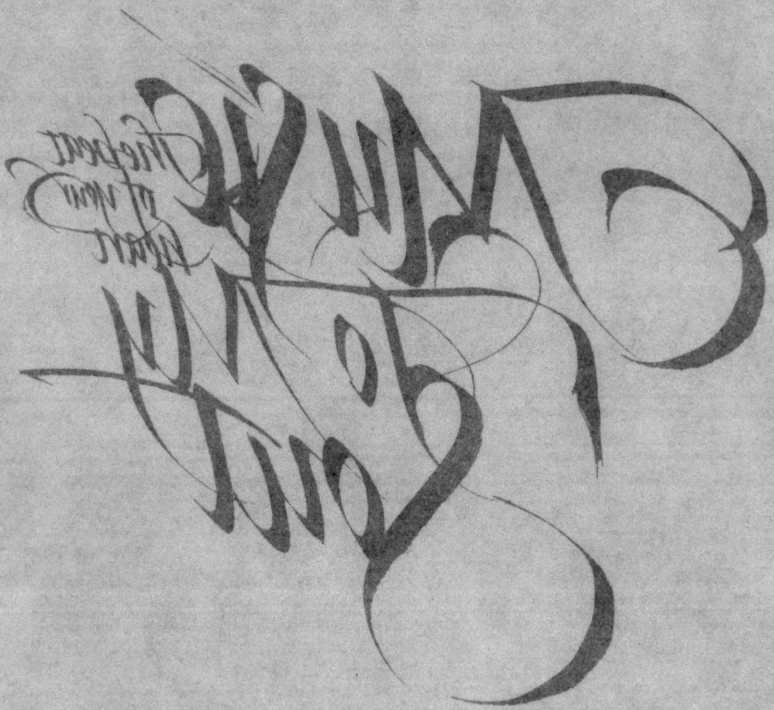

SWEET MUSIC

Lying close
Experiencing
Your peaceful face
Your rhythmic breathing
The beat
Of your heart
The smell
Of your skin
The warmth
Of your breath
The gentle rise and fall
Of your chest
Under my hand
As you drift
Off to sleep
Music
To my Soul

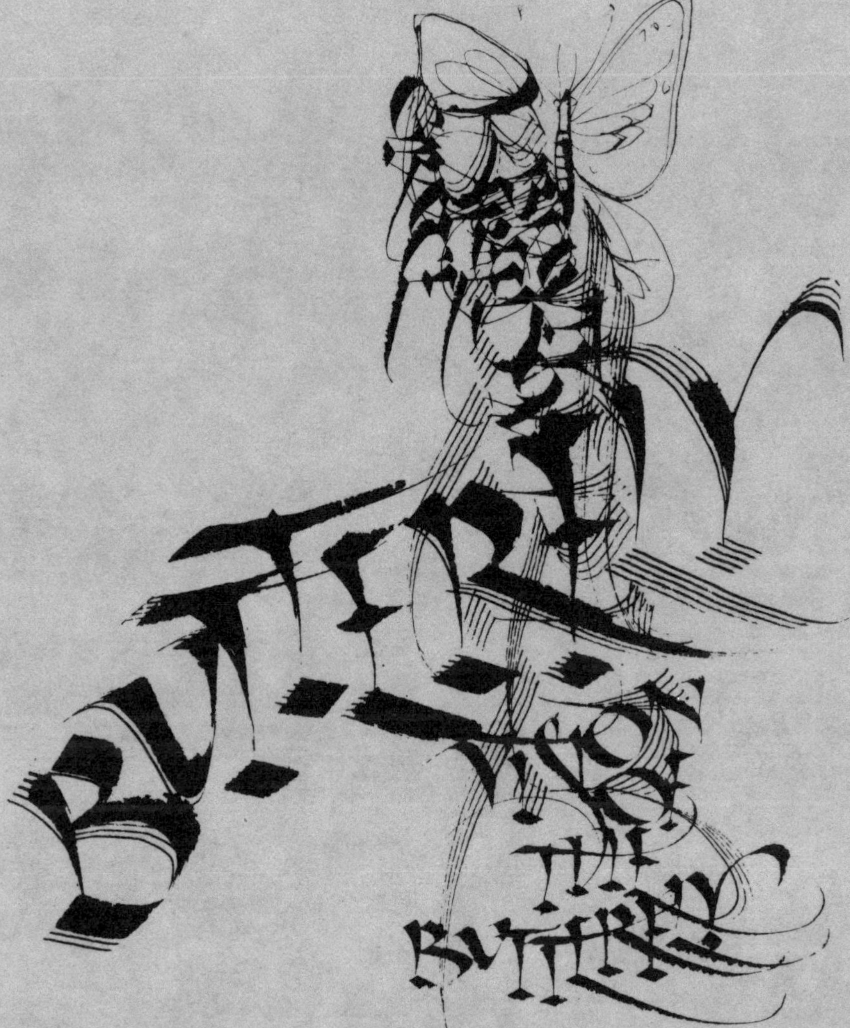

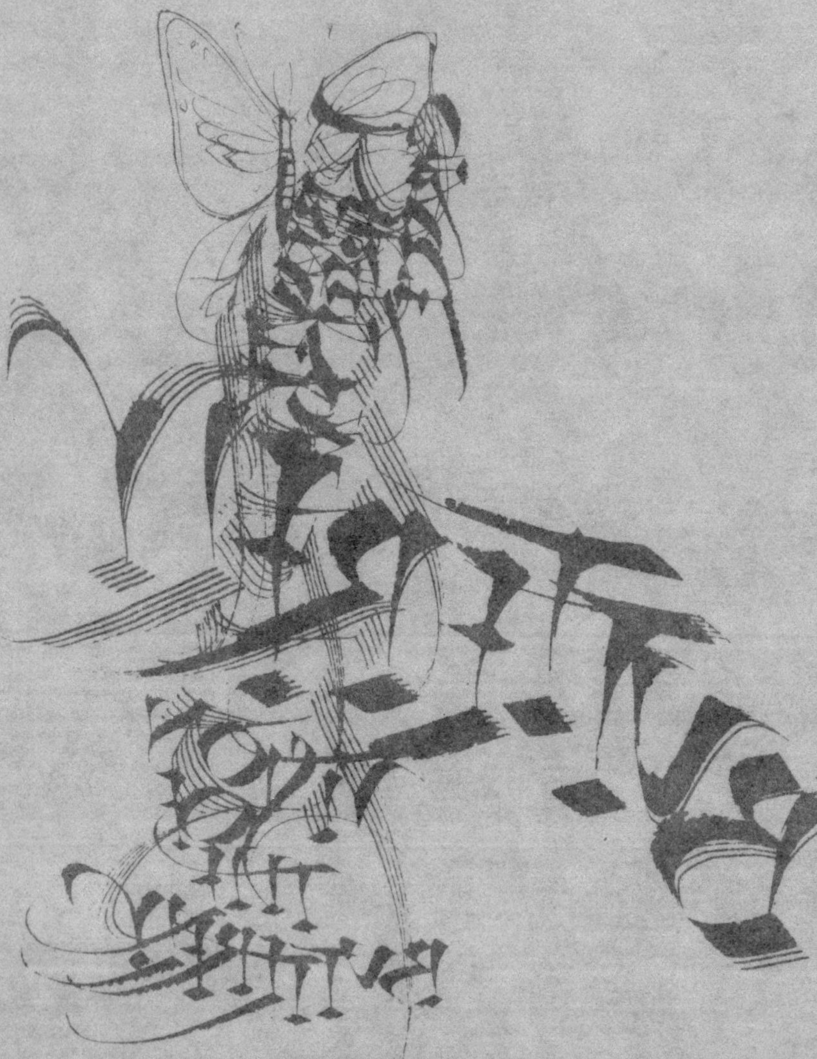

BUTTERFLY

Butterfly
Fly free
Be free
Supreme beauty
Delicate
Perfect
Too beautiful
To capture
To hold
The heart beholds
The wonder
Of perfect Love
Beautiful in its freedom
Behold its grace
Experience its purity
Its timeless beauty exists
In perfect freedom
And lives
In the hearts and minds
Of two who share
The vision of
The butterfly

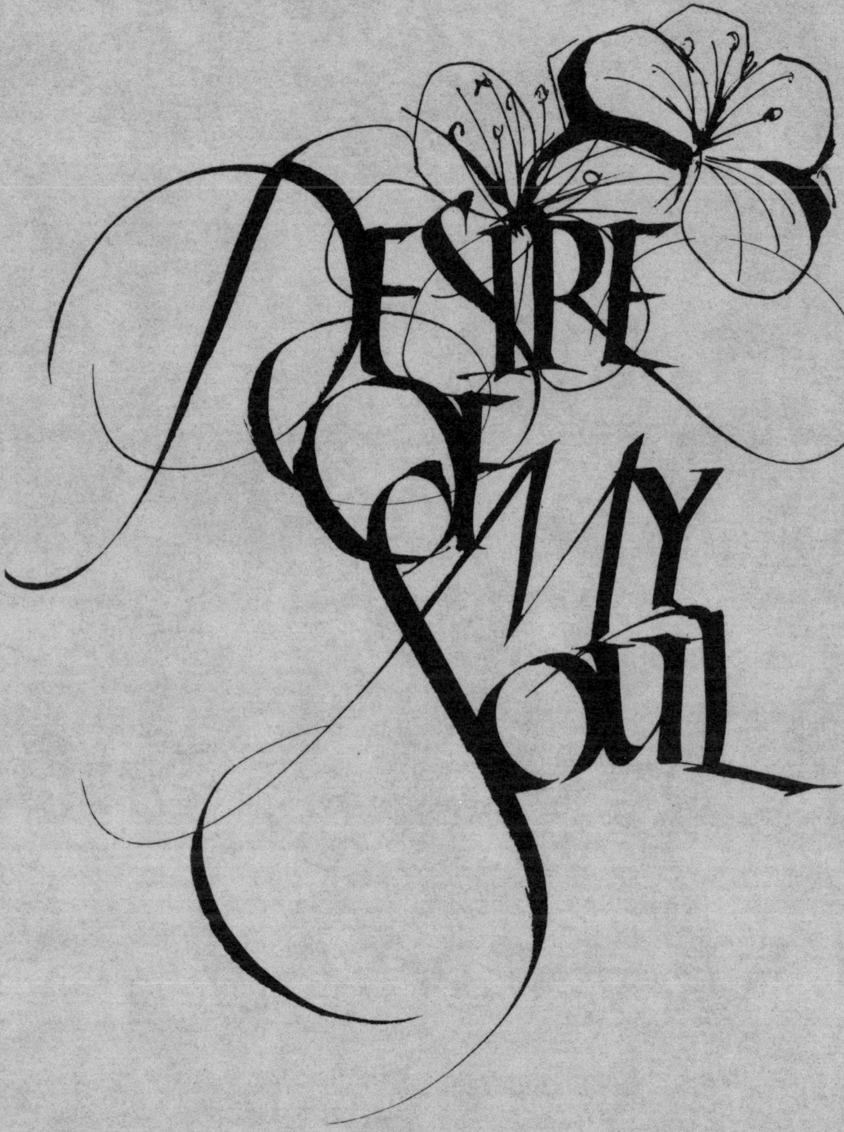
Desire of My Soul

Desire of my Soul
Intensely burning
A touch
A look
Drinking deeply
The essence of you.
The memory of two
Rising in fire,
From the warmth
Of a spark.
The miracle of life
Passion's dream
Never ends,
Lives again,
Nevers dies.
Light of my Soul
Love of my life
Evermore

He was always here
No beginning
&
No end

He leaves
But is not gone
Don't ask
From where he came
He was always here
No beginning
And no end
Of my Soul
One and all

No beginning No end No beginning No end

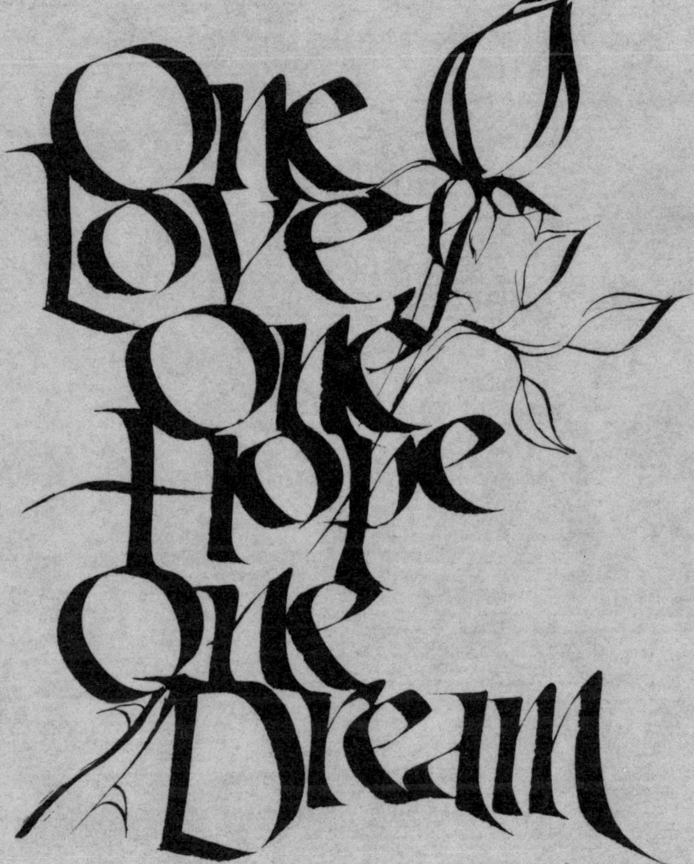
One
Love
One
Hope
One
Dream

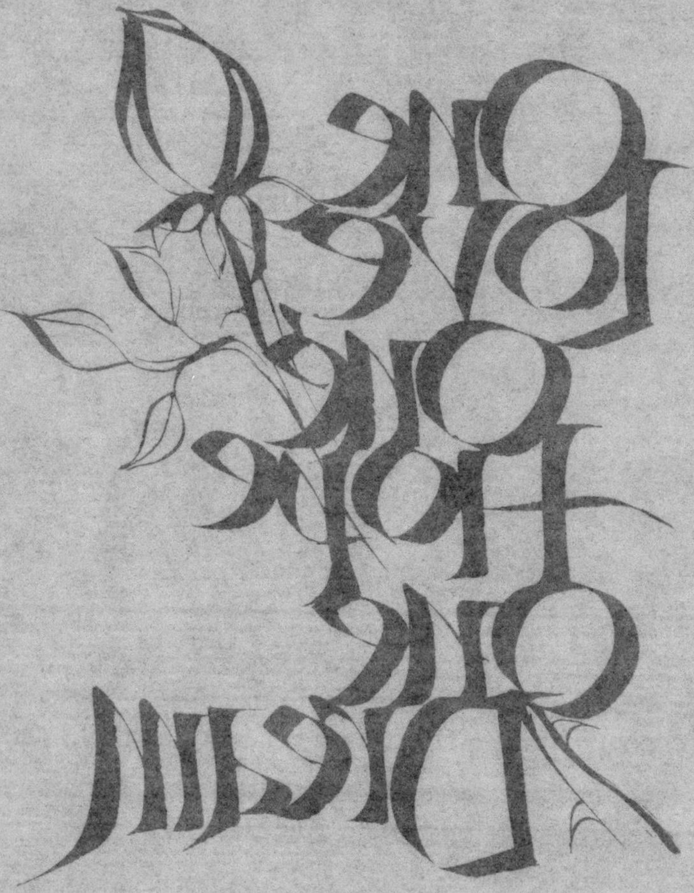

Tender Love
And growing trust
Abide with us
Each day

Apart or near
Our passion grows
One Love, One Hope
One Dream

Precious one
My Prince of Love
Be all that
You can be

Life's sweeter still
Each blessed day
Because, My Love,
You are

My
PRAYER

Share your
whole life
with
me

My
PRAYER

My
PRAYER

My
PRAYER

Talk with me
Laugh with me
Play with me
Be with me
Be like a child with me

Teach me
And love me
Walk through this world with me
Ever be near me
Share your whole life with me
Always be there

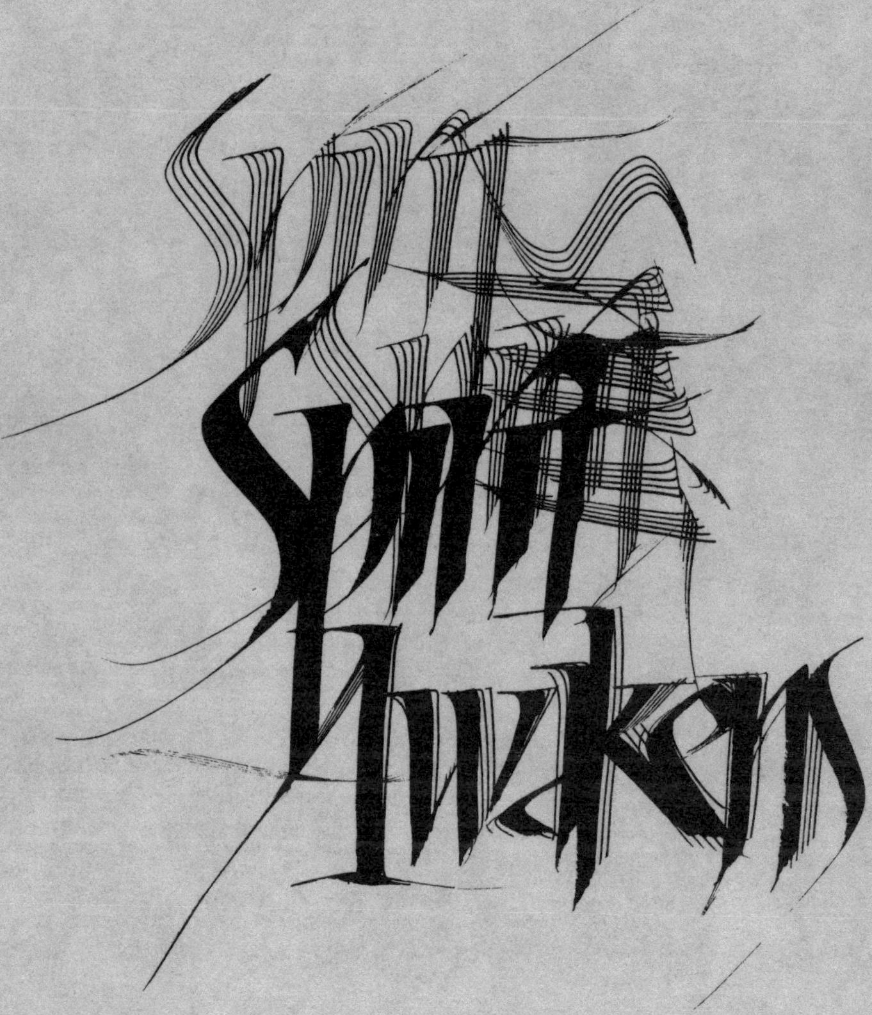

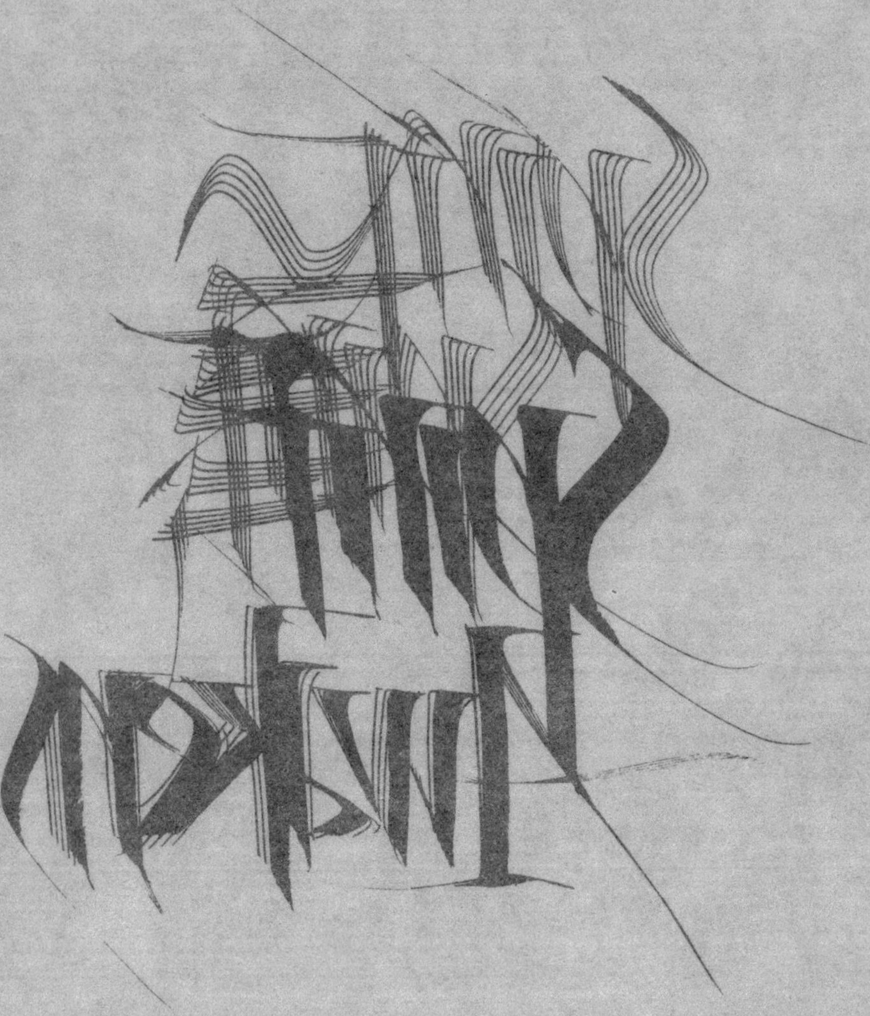

My spirit awakens
In the wonder of you
My body enlivens
As memories shine through
Thank God for our passion
Pleasure shared by two
God's Love abides with us
Heavenly gift
Given in truth

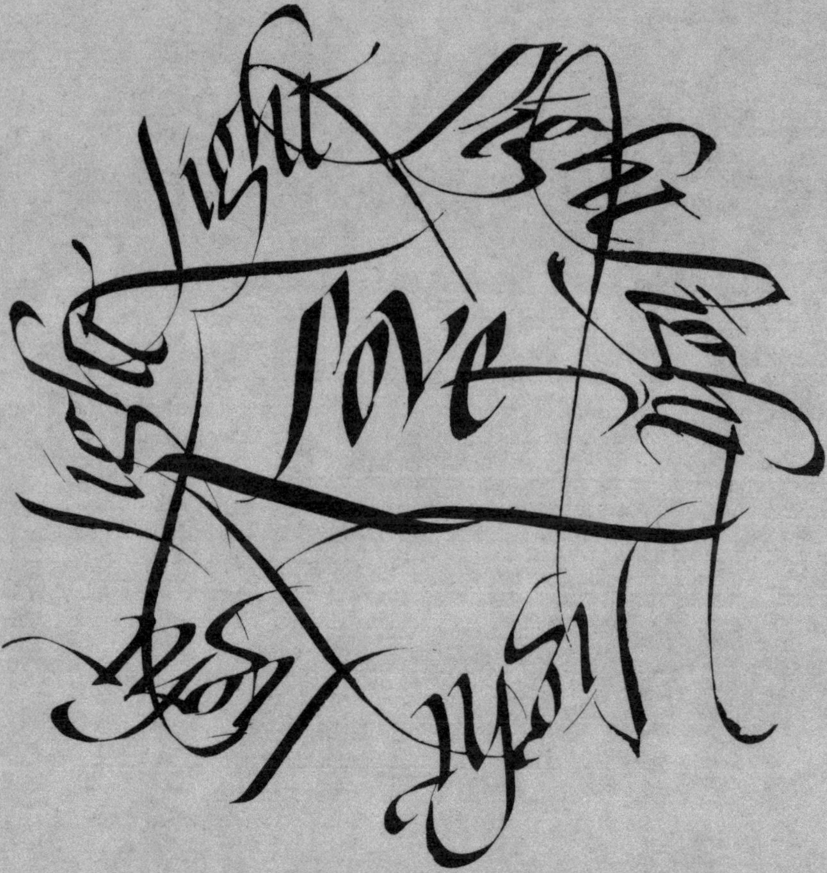
light
Love

ONE LIGHT

Two worlds
Apart
Two souls
One Love
No time
No space
Two minds
One thought
Together
While apart
Peace
No fear
One Light
No darkness
Everlasting
And eternal
Love
Pure Love

Our Spirits Fly So High

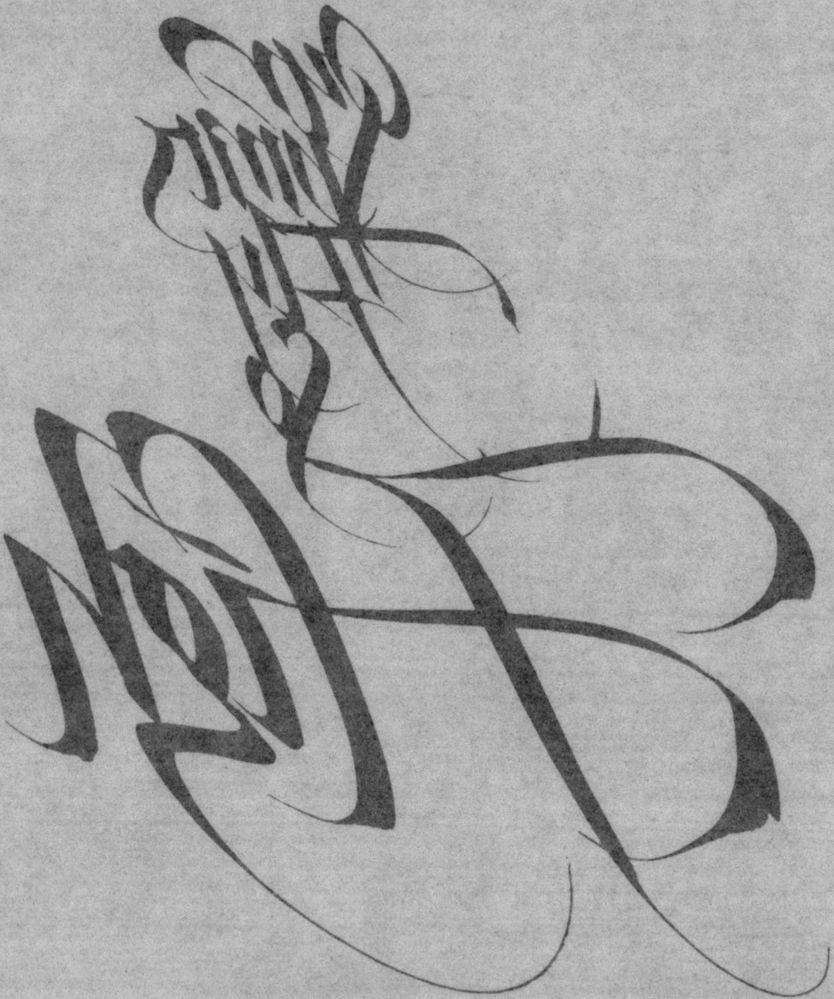

SO HIGH

Beyond
All earthly bonds
Our spirits
Fly
So high

Within
Two lovers share
One Love
Fire
So high

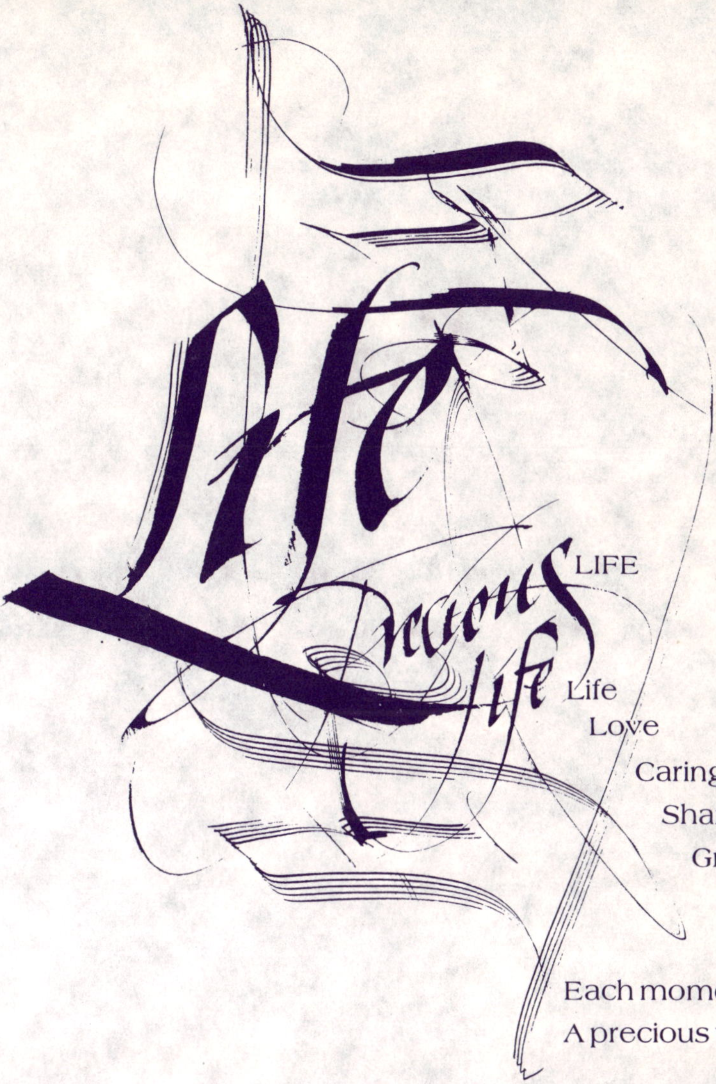

LIFE

Life
Love
Caring
Sharing
Growing
Love

Each moment of life,
A precious wonder

To be experienced
To be shared

Precious Life

In love
I have
power
with God
Co-
Creator
all is possible
To serve
AND
to love

This love that I feel
Is bigger than me
It flows through my Soul
In each cell, all around me
My purpose is clear
To Love and to teach
To learn and to grow
In Love I have power
Co-Creator with God
To serve and to Love
Everyone
Everything
That is His

The Treasures of Your Mind & Your Soul

You opened the door

You invited me in

You shared

The treasures

Of your mind

And your soul

SPIRIT
OF THE WIND
SPIRIT
OF THE SUN
SPIRIT
OF THE EARTH
SPIRIT
OF ETERNAL
LOVE

Spirit of the wind
Blow my cares away
Breathe me with your Light
Every night and day

Spirit of the sun
Warm me, give me Light
Fill my life with Love
Throughout eternity

Spirit of the earth
Mother of us all
Feed my blessed Soul
With miracle of life

Spirit of eternal Love
Keep me warm and safe
Fill my Soul, That I may be
A servant all my days

Rise Toward the Light

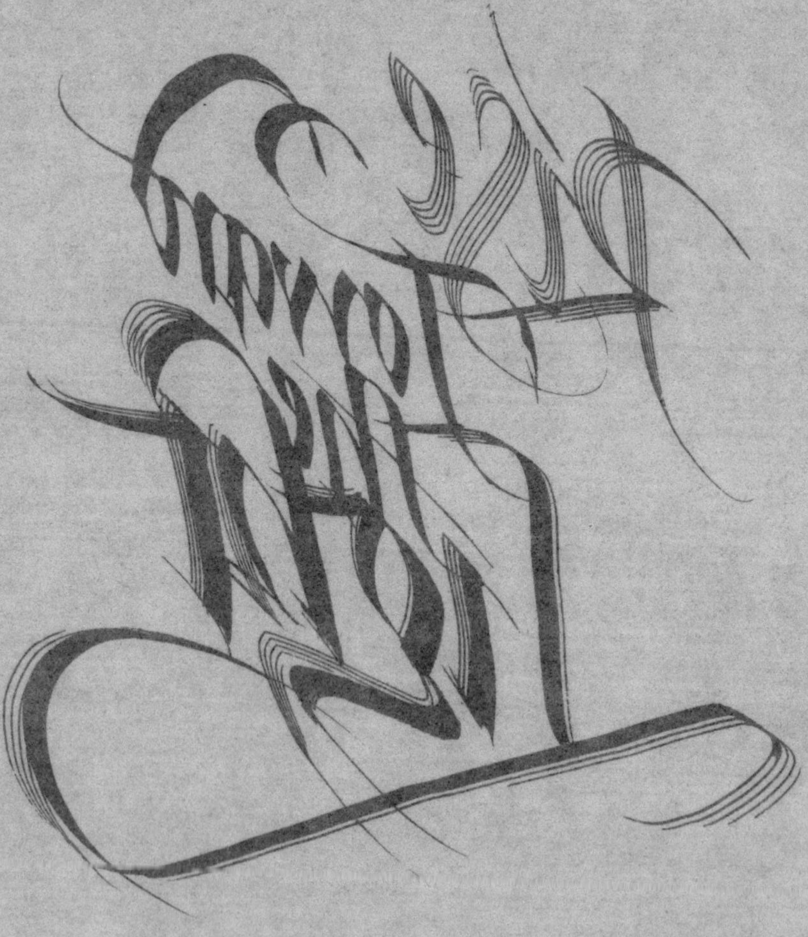

Sharing
Caring
Wonder of Life
Being
Feeling
Joy in the flight
Talking
Touching
One in the night
Loving
Knowing
Rise toward the Light

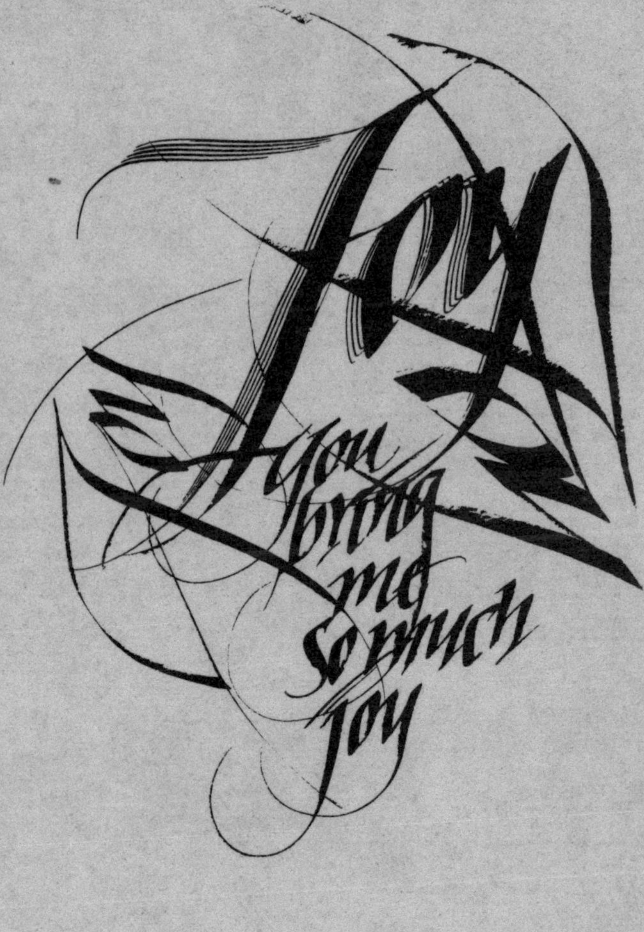
Joy
You
bring
me
So much
Joy

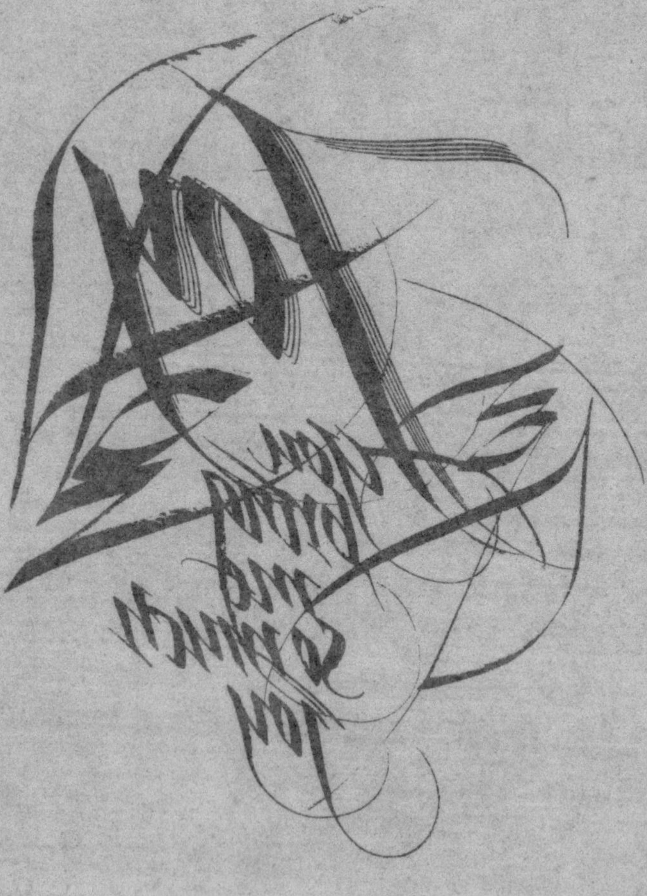

You bring me so much joy
My Love flows on and on
Your smile, your eyes
Your loving touch
Bring peace unto my Soul.

My life is filled
Beyond my dreams
My grateful heart
Pours forth
Praise to God
His gifts we share
Throughout Eternity.

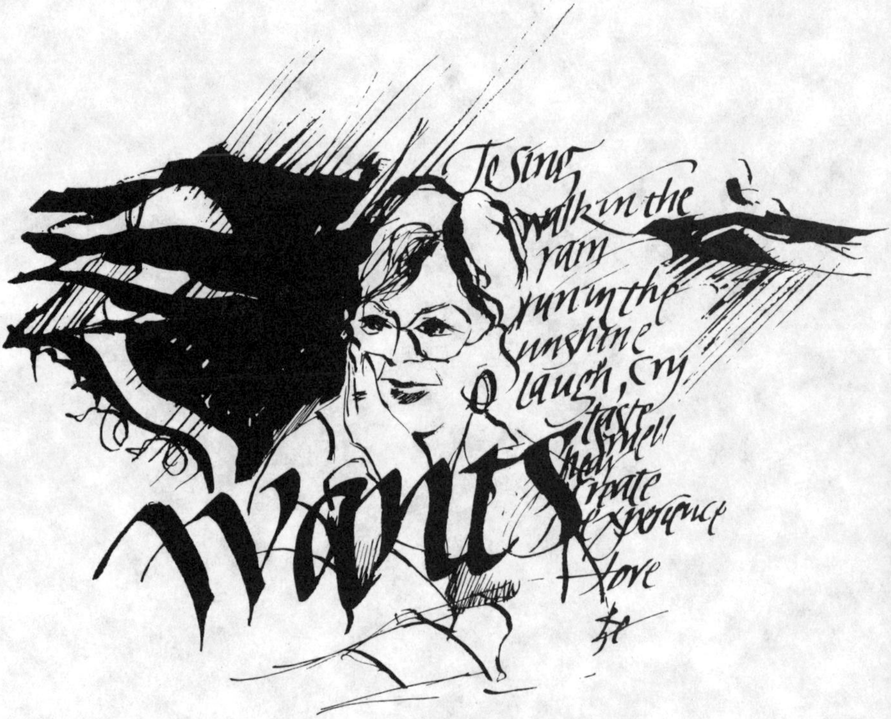

I WANT

I want
To sing
To walk in the rain
To run in the sunshine
To laugh, to cry
To taste, to smell, to hear
To play
To create
To feel
To experience
To love
To be

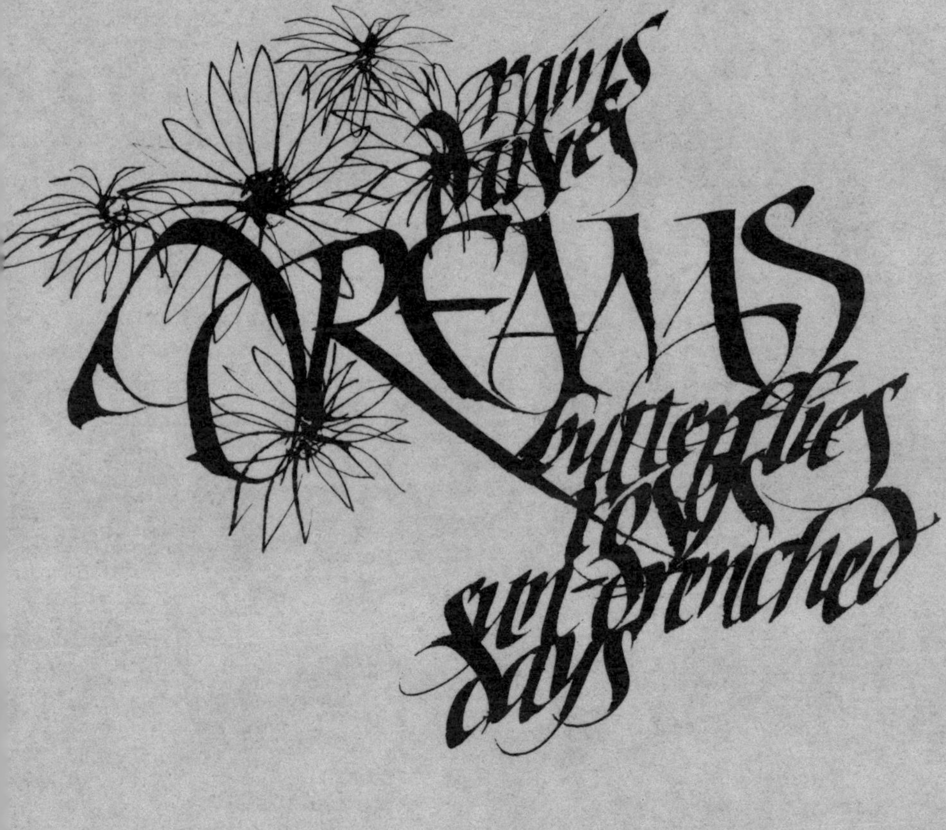
rains
daisies
DREAMS
butterflies
love
sun drenched
days

I DREAM

I dream of
Sun-drenched days
Cool sandy shores
Star-filled nights
How could I want more?

Warm summer rains
Crisp winter snow
Puddles and daisies
Butterflies, a rose.

Walking beside you
Laughter and tears
Loving you dearly
Through all our years.

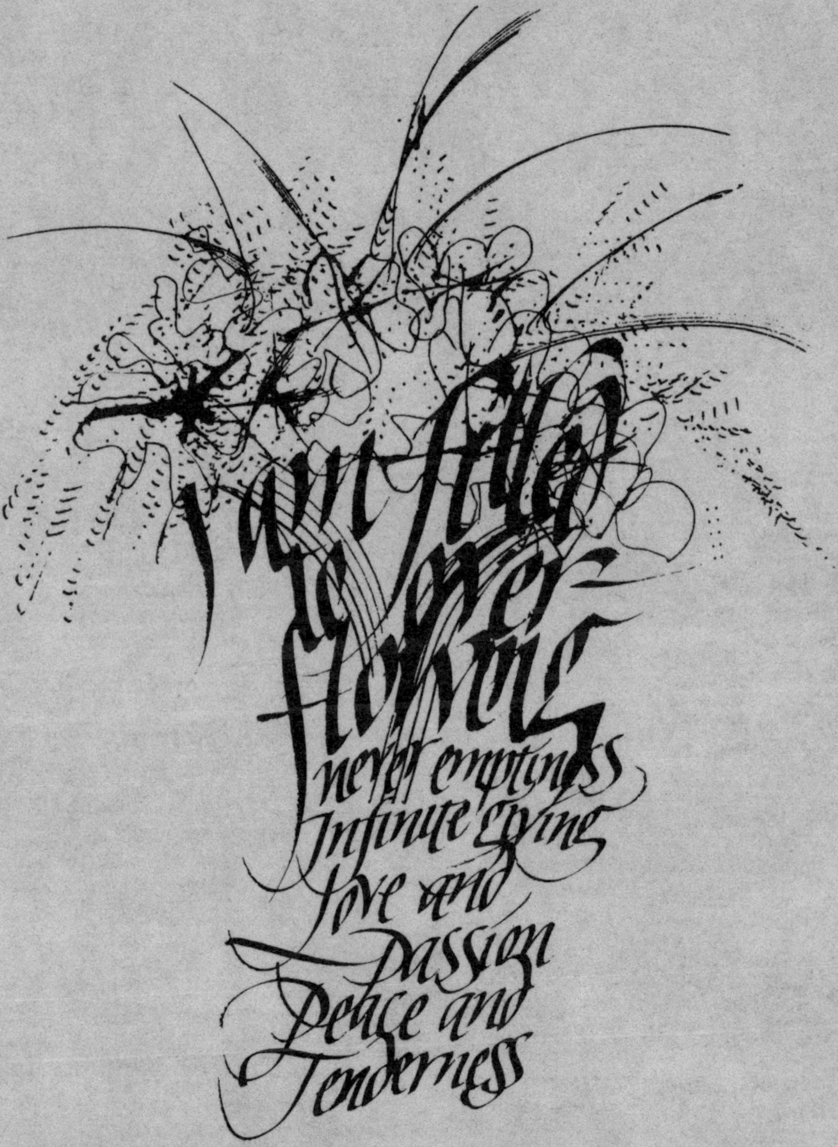
I am filled
to over
flowing
never emptiness
Infinite giving
love and
passion
peace and
tenderness

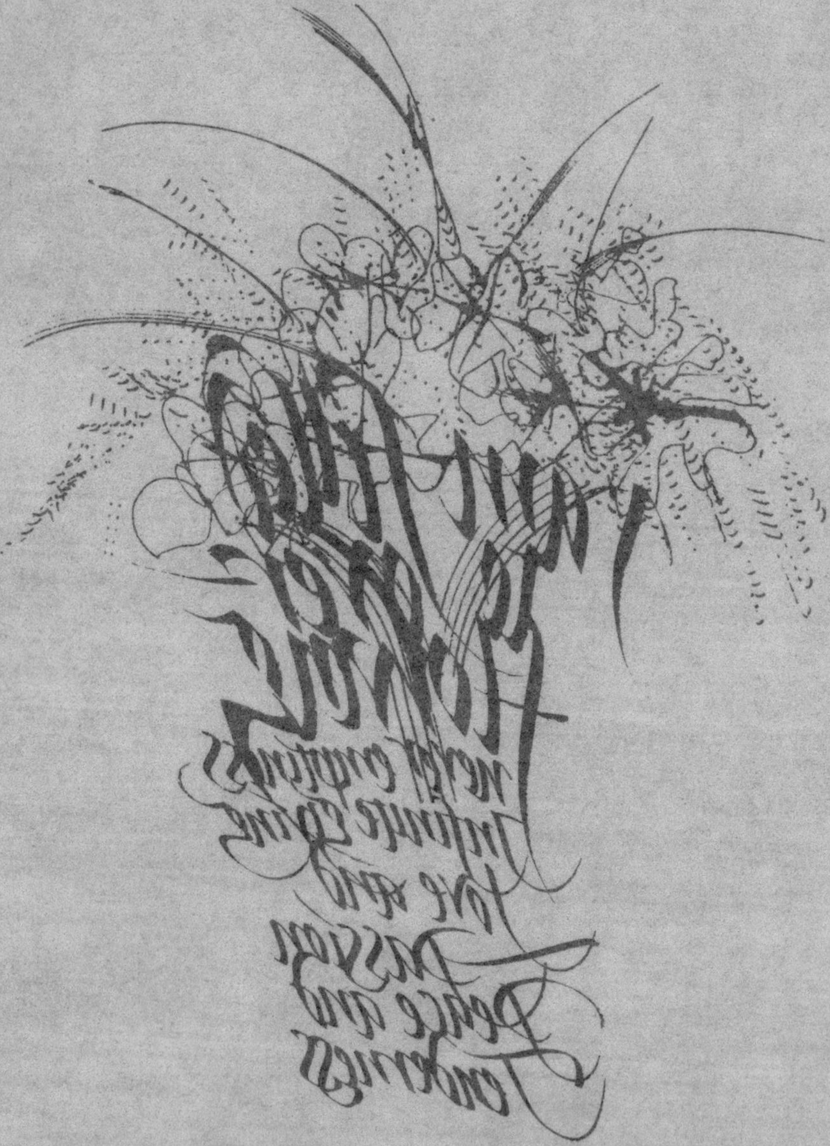

I am filled
To overflowing
Never emptiness
No need
Infinite giving
Love and passion
Peace and tenderness
Fills my Soul
And I am blessed
Never-ending
Ever-flowing
Forever
And
Beyond

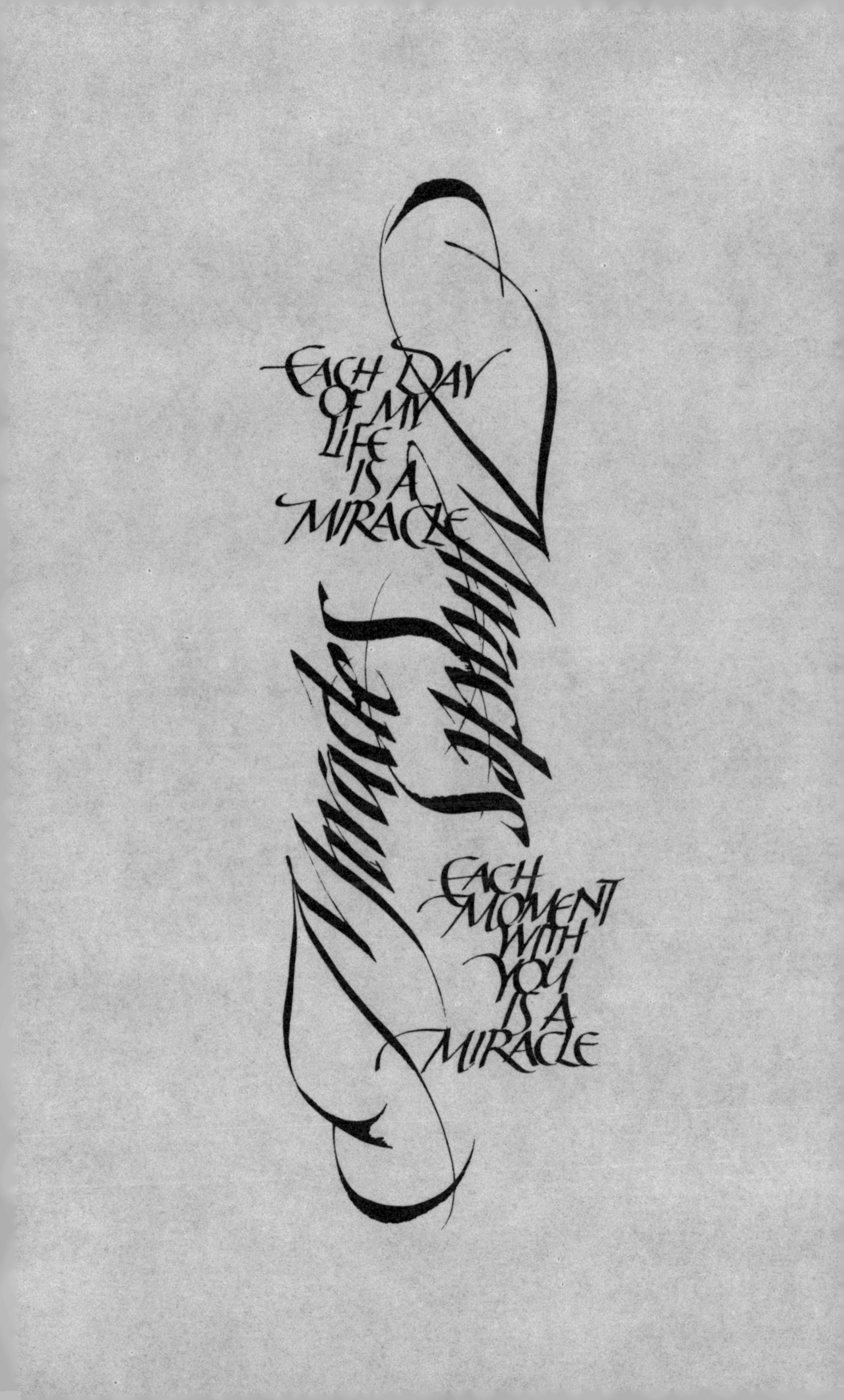

EACH DAY
OF MY
LIFE
IS A
MIRACLE

EACH
MOMENT
WITH
YOU
IS A
MIRACLE

A MIRACLE

Each day of my life
Is a miracle
A gift from God
One more day
    To create
        To enjoy
            To love
Each breath that I take
Is a miracle
A gift from God
One more breath
    To receive
        To treasure
            To love
Each moment with you
Is a miracle
A gift from God
One more chance
    To experience
        To enjoy
            To love
Each thought of you
Is a miracle
A gift from God
One more chance
    To be
        To know
            To feel you near

Gems of Wisdom

Gems of Wisdom

By a Knight who slew
a few dragons of perception
and opened a gate
to a new kingdom
so I could explore
the lands
of enchantment
and wonder.

Eyes wide open,
the Knight laid before me
Gems of Wisdom,
a treasure of gleaming
facets, windows
and views to new worlds
within my own.

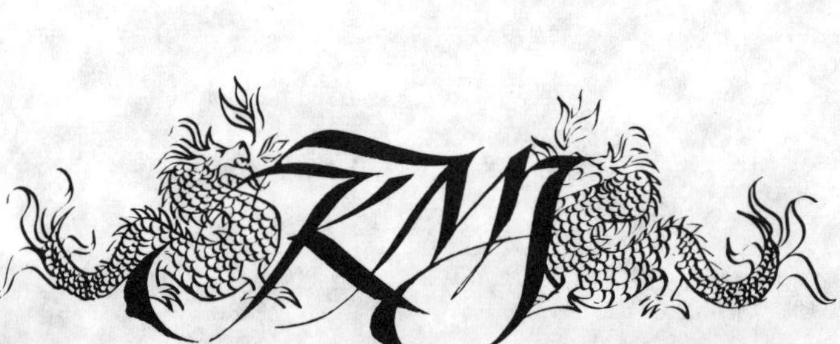

You have given me
gems of wisdom which
I hold in my heart--
I continue to polish them
and the facets are continuing
to sparkle with more light.
You have brought me
to the Light.

"ELEVEN"

Whenever I am asked "Can I ask you a question?" I always respond "Eleven!". "What?" they say, and I say "Eleven! That's my standard answer to all questions." "You see Eleven is the answer to all of our questions. It represents you and me. See, I am one and you are one. If we become dependent upon one another then the sum of one and one is only two. But if we remain independent, yet supportive and giving, we stand on our own, and next to each other. We must be independent and inter-dependent so that our individual values, supporting and giving to each other, create more than the sum of our dependence. In this fashion, one next to one equals Eleven. A greater sum than the dependent combining of our individual selves. Eleven means we stand independent as individuals, yet together, side by side a greater power than the sum of the two. Never losing identity, but also creating a greater force by our combined spirits and supporting the individual efforts".

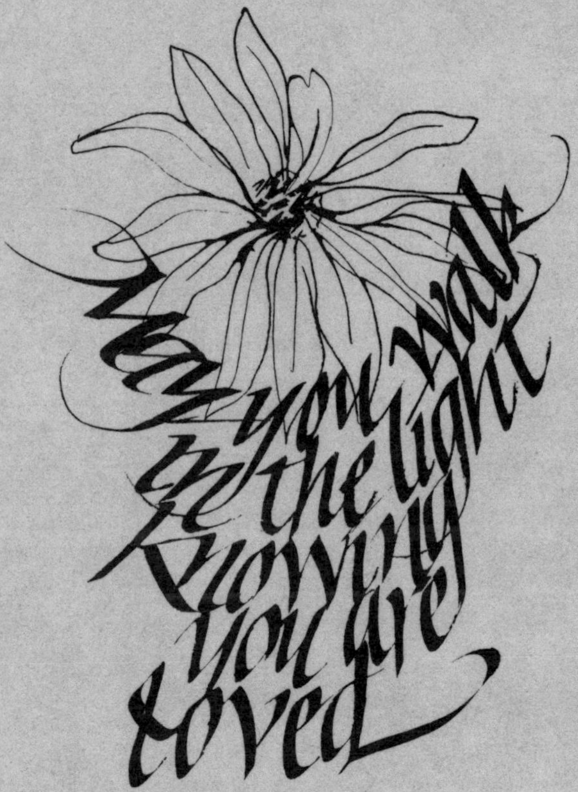
May you walk
in the light
knowing
you are
loved

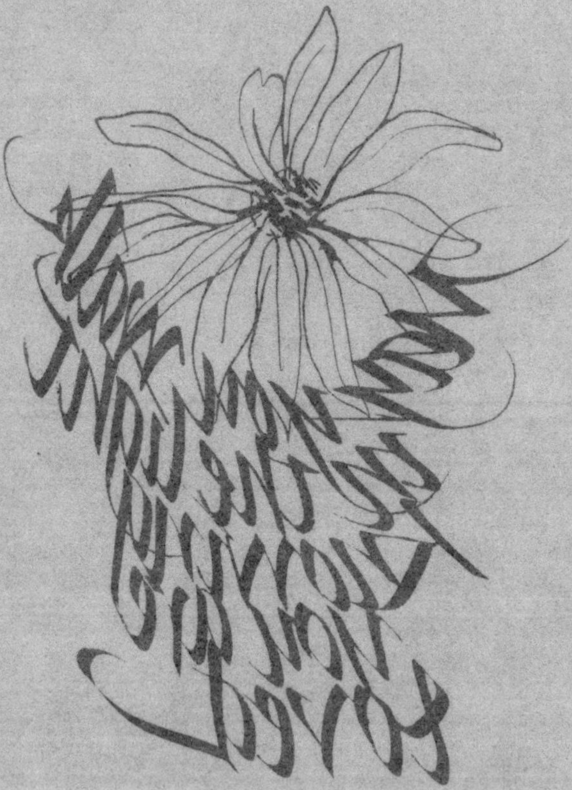

Life is a struggle
While we are in this human body.
It will be a struggle
Until we die
We have lessons to learn
You are one of the few who understand
You are beautiful
You are loved.

I know it's been a tough time.

Relax . . .
Everything is going to be fine . . .
Have faith and trust . . . I know you
are going to do wonders. It's been
a challenge . . . Through challenges
we grow, we learn. Remember,
through a lot of the pressures . . .
We help get our "filthy" coal pressed
to making a beautiful diamond . . .
Then some of the friction, some of the
wearing and rubbing creates the facets
on that diamond so that you can
capture the Light . . . Feel the warmth
and glow . . . And glow yourself . . .
As you radiate like the diamond.

Hang in there, OK!

In the center of the storm is the calm. Move with the storm--have faith and let go of those things you can't control.

Feel the peace of the calm; feel when you might be swept into the storm and get back to the center.

Trust in Divine Order . . . Let go!

Don't be perfect.
Otherwise, you remove our humanity.
There is only one perfect One.
The nature of humanity
is that we are imperfect.
Remain human, for in all our frailties
we find lessons in life
and appreciation for living.

You are loved and cherished

FORGIVE YOURSELF

We waste so much time punishing ourselves and never forgiving ourselves, that we never heal from the issue. Put a rubber band around your wrist. Every time you feel you must beat yourself up because you cannot forgive yourself, give the rubber band a good snap. That "ouch" will be your punishment, then let it go and forgive yourself.

It's OK to make mistakes,
"Cause we're only HUMAN after all."

You are a professional;

More than that,

You are a Wonderful professional.

You are the best!

Do not fret about a job or getting employment,

You are employed; you are a consultant,

you have 3 clients . . . "Me, Myself and I"

First and foremost you are serving and

working for yourself. By providing

to others you are providing for yourself.

Take care of your clients and customers

and you take care of yourself.

I do not own you;
I do not possess you;
Therefore
I can not lose you.

You are gold.
You are shining.
You are brilliant.

You are a little girl in a beautiful
flower garden--There are no
spiders in your garden.

Be calm and enjoy the WONDER!

Look at your diamond;
How long did it take the earth
To make that diamond?
You are becoming a diamond!

The earth forms diamonds by exerting
great heat, tremendous pressure and
unbelievable forces to compress dark,
black, soft coal into nature's hardest
natural substance, diamonds.
You too are shaped and compressed by
tremendous stresses and pressures of life.
This heat, and unbelievable force help
you to become like a diamond.

A beautiful, clear, light gathering and
reflective, multi-faceted person,
Full of Fire and Brilliance.

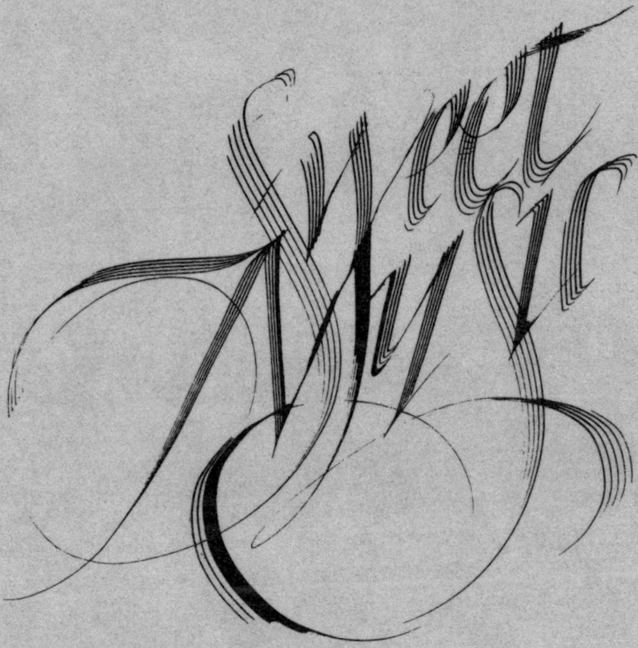
Sweet Music

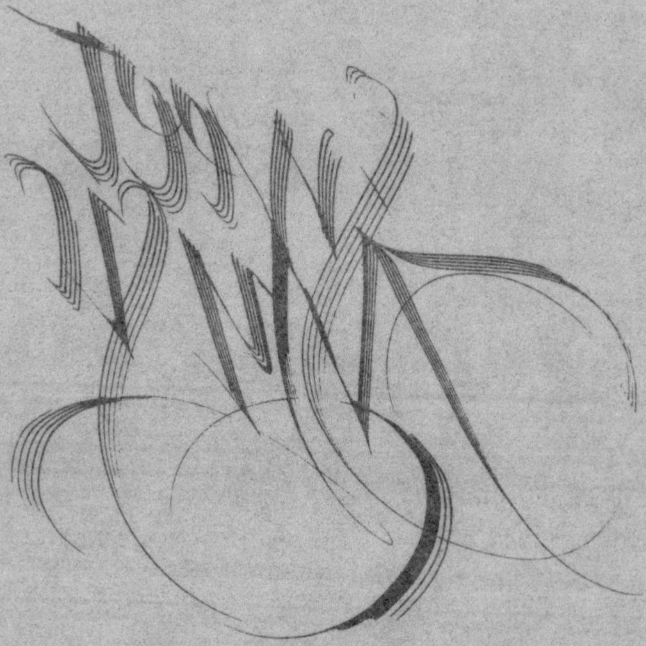

You are wonderful; you bring out the best in people and they bring out the best in you. Synergy.

The energy is flowing!

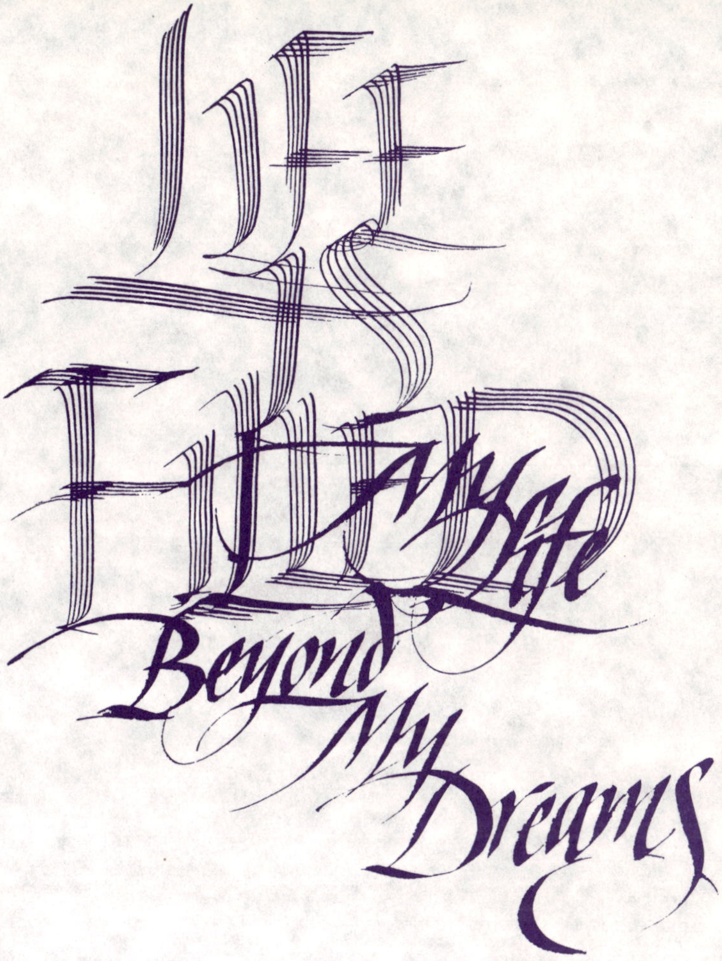

ONE
LIGHT
ONE
LOVE

SHARON
WARREN

PROUDLY PRODUCED IN OREGON

Design by Letters & Lines Graphics - Tualatin
Camera work by:
Chehalem Printing - Newberg
B-Laser Graphics - Portland
Printed by Printistry - McMinnville
Foil/Emboss by Liepelt & Son - Portland
Bound by Oregon Book Binding - Silverton